BEGIN
BELIEVE
BECOME

EDWARD JULIAN

© 2015, First Edition

The Begin Within Initiative, LLC

All rights reserved.

No portion of this book may be copied, stored, or transmitted in any form without prior written consent of the publisher, except for brief quotations used in reviews, articles, or critical analysis.

This work reflects the real-life journey and experiences of Edward A. Julian, Sr. The events, emotions, and reflections are presented exactly as lived by the author.

Created and published by

The Begin Within Initiative, LLC

Columbus, Ohio

Email: beginbelievebecome14@gmail.com

Website: www.edwardajuliansr.com

ISBN-10: 0692417753

ISBN-13: 978-0692417751

Printed in the United States of America

Every page is a reminder that your past does not define your future—it prepares you for it.

Acknowledgements

This book is dedicated to my wife, Giena Julian for her support and encouragement. When others said I couldn't, you said I could. When others said I wouldn't, you said I would. When others turned their backs on me, you turned around and put your back up against mine. The only time you turned around was to tell me everything would be fine.

This book is also dedicated to my mother, Marjorie. I love you. Because of the poem you gave me as a young man, "Don't Quit" by Ralph Acosta, I'm making a difference in my life and the lives of others.

TABLE OF CONTENTS

Acknowledgements v
   Believe in You ix
   By EJ 2015 ix
INTRODUCTION xii
BEGIN 1
   Know Thy Self (Personal Inventory) 21
   Poem: Rise and Fall 23
   By EJ 2013 23
BELIEVE 26
   BELIEVE IN YOU! 29
   Know Thy Self (Personal Inventory) 37
   Blessin' Blockin' 38
   Poem by EJ 2013 38
BECOME 41
   What is the opposite of success? 46
   I HAD TO DO THE WORK. 48
   I HAD TO PUT IN THE WORK. 49
   IT COULD BE WORSE. 53
   Know Thy Self (Personal Inventory) 53

Poem: My Life..55
Poem by EJ 2014 55
Thank You **58**

Believe in You
By EJ 2015

Never settle for less

Just being you makes you the best

Respect starts with you

Many are called but the chosen are few

Channel your pride,

Face your fears inside.

The depths of your struggle can't be denied,

Pushing against what is.

As a man thinks so he is,

A glimmer of hope is all you need,

With the faith of a mustard seed.

The jealous clouds may swallow the sun,

The moon alters its shape for fun,

Life is about change,

Nothing ever stays the same.

Some days you are up, some days you are down,

It's who you become when the next day rolls around

People will talk

Have different opinions of you

It's not who they think you are

But the things you say & don't do

Where there is life, there is hope.

And you should never take your life for a joke,

If the mind can conceive it,

The man can achieve it

Nothing is too small to know

Nothing is too big to attempt & grow

Success is a journey not a destination

Relax and let it flow

Never hold your head low

Let the sidewalk fall victim

A man becomes a man

But not by the people who picked him.

This is your true awakening

Your chance to be free

Don't expect to be what you haven't worked to be

INTRODUCTION

I will be the first to admit that I did a lot of wrong in my life, including running the streets and chasing a false reality. However, after being released from prison and working at a homeless shelter in Cleveland, then finding a full---time job in Columbus, Ohio and now, working as a mentor for at---risk youth and individuals who are transitioning from incarceration, I **believe** along the way I also did something right.

These experiences have taught me that life is 10% what happens to you and 90% how you react to it.

I'm not going to tell you anything you don't already know. After being incarcerated for 14 years, I'm sure there's actually much you could teach me. I can only tell you what I know, what I've been through, and how I've learned to never give up no matter what I've been up against. Despite the challenges I faced and the obstacles I had to overcome, I pushed forward, saying to myself, "This too shall pass."

Every one of us has a story to tell, and every single one of us has a past.

- *Are you ashamed of your past?*
- *Do you have a past you don't want to share with others?*

I ask because I have a past that I used to be embarrassed to share, but these days, I'm experiencing a great joy telling people I was incarcerated for 14 years. I believe if I help change at least one person's life, then the 14 years I spent in prison was well worth it. When I look back at my childhood and reflect on my life, I remember the things I wanted to be. Unfortunately, I became more of the things I didn't want to be. Growing up, I wanted to be a model. I wanted to be an educator. I wanted to be a personal trainer and a fitness coach. I wanted to be a professional basketball player. Most of all, I wanted to be a father to my children. And yet, instead of becoming the man and father I wanted to be, I moved further away from all the aspirations I had for myself. I moved further from that man, further from that father.

For 14 years, I was the picture of everything a father should not be. I was a male, but not the man I thought I was. Frederick Douglas once said, "Men may not get all they pay for in this world, but they certainly pay for all they get." When I look back, I can see all the wrong payments I made, all the bad checks I wrote, all the pain I endured, all the mistakes and bad choices, and all the hard times I suffered.

The criminal justice system labeled me a three-time convicted felon. Society said I was a three---time loser, but after readjusting myself and reinventing my life, I can now say I am a three---time survivor!

I want you to remember that someone's opinion of you does not have to become your reality. Never let someone's diagnosis become your prognosis.

Don't let other people's stereotypes, needs, desires, fantasies, fears, goals, or dreams dictate your choices, views, and decisions. Follow your own path. Blaze your own trail. Do not worry if people say you are being selfish, disloyal, dishonest, or narcissistic. You cannot please everyone. You will never make everyone happy. People will talk about you whether you are doing good or bad, right or wrong.

No matter what people say or do, no matter what change life brings your way, hold your values and be honest with yourself. When everyone and everything is changing around you, be willing, from the heart, to embrace the process of being restored, retrained, reshaped, and renewed. Just make sure your intentions are good and with no malice, and your actions meet up with your expressed interest.

People will talk and have different opinions of you; however, it's not just the things you say, but things you say and don't do.

BEGIN

Edward A. Julian Sr.

Basketball was my escape from the terrible side of the truth. I was poor, uneducated, misunderstood, misguided, and influenced by the streets. Basketball was my safe haven when I had nothing and no one to talk to or depend on. When I placed a ball in my hand, I felt like the gazelle running from the lion of my painful reality.

No matter how many times I ran to basketball for that shield of protection, the game felt like more of a band---aid on a bigger problem. I was trapped in this false reality where I believed basketball was not the answer because it did not improve my circumstances. In that reality that I was living, basketball felt like a temporary safe haven. I believed my social conditions were chasing me, like a gazelle being chased by a lion. It was my state of mind that made me vulnerable, and the lifestyle of the streets was a strong predator pursuing me. So, I turned to selling drugs, and I became the lion in this false reality. Selling drugs provided the money and power to "fix" my social conditions for the time. I thought I was living normal, but I was not operating under normal thinking.

To begin a process of change, you have to know why you want to change. You have to have a why. Today, My why is staying out of prison and avoiding the circumstances that could cause me to be incarcerated again. My why is my mother and all the lessons she taught me. My why is living out her legacy. My why is being a father to my five children. My why is my community because of the some of the damage I caused in the past, and I want to help make it better.

Once you have your why, you have got to be careful because it is easy to start second---guessing yourself and your course of action. Once you have your why, you cannot focus on the challenges. Instead, you have to focus on the getting busy making the changes. Like an athlete training for a competition, you have to work until you cannot do anymore. You have no time to question or worry. You have to give it your all without giving up. It can be easier to focus on how far you have to go to accomplish your aspirations instead of how far you have already come.

Now that I know my why, I can begin my journey towards embracing my past, changing my future, and being more like the bold lion pursuing my dreams.

...

Acceptance ⟶ Forgiveness

- **Are you backing down more than you are standing up?**
- **Do you love *you* for who you are and what you have *become*?**

Now, I want you to forget all the reasons why you have backed down in the past. Forget all the reasons you have given up on your goals and dreams. **Believe** in the one reason you can make a difference and a change in your life today.

I want you to stop beating yourself up over what you have not **become** and **begin** by taking the first step to accept yourself as you are now. The past cannot be changed, but the future is determined by how you think and act today. Accept your mistakes, no matter how bad they are. You have to accept your present reality without guilt or judgment in order to move past it and make the changes you want.

Trust me. I know firsthand how challenging it is to be stuck in a rut when your life is upside----down, and you feel like everyone has given up on you. I know how it feels to be broke with no money and broken inside, fearing the unknown. I've been there, especially when I didn't know how I was going to deal with the future upon my release from prison. Even now, at times, I feel like I'm trapped because of my criminal history.

Starting over isn't easy, and forgiving others can be even harder. Nothing in life is easy. Everything you do in life takes time, energy, and patience. Everything in life is a process. A baby learns to crawl before he can walk. If you start a new job, it is going to take time to be trained, to earn people's trust before you can expect a promotion. You cannot look at other people who are ahead of you and expect to have what they have. It takes time. You have to put in the effort. You may need to go to college and get a degree to achieve what you want. That takes time and work. If your why is worth it to you, it will require commitment especially when things get tough.

If you do what is easy, your life will be hard.
If you do what is hard, your life will be easy.

So, let's take the first step to change. Let's take the first step toward readjusting and reinventing ourselves.

How do you do that?

Acceptance and forgiveness.

When you forgive yourself, you confirm who you are today—the good, the bad, and the ugly. You take ownership of your mistakes, bad judgments, and bad decisions from the past.

One of my favorite books says "He without sin cast the first stone."

One sin is not greater than the other. If you steal a penny, but someone else steals a thousand dollars, it is still stealing, and it is still a sin. A drug dealer is no worse than a corrupt judge. A thief is no better than a liar. A sin is a sin. Wrong is wrong. You cannot right a wrong by doing wrong. You right a wrong by forgiving. First, you must forgive yourself, and then you must forgive others.

Forgiving yourself is the most important step.

Why?

Because though you have forgiven yourself, you will learn that others, even your family and friends, may not, and that is okay. Sometimes you may have to forgive others before you can forgive yourself.

Forgiving others gives you a chance to make amends for the wrongs and heartaches you caused in their life, so don't worry if they still blame you for things that happen in their life. Don't worry if they still hold a grudge. Forgive them anyways. Forgive them for your own peace of mind. You will prove your sincerity through your forgiveness of them and through your actions and deeds.

For example, I may have hurt you in the past, but I may not have opportunity to apologize and make things right, so I apologize by doing the next best thing. I apologize by doing the right thing to other people. I apologize by giving back to my community. I apologize by being kind to other people. Maybe over time if you are an open----minded person, you will be able to forgive me.

Keep in mind, though, that not everybody is going to be on board with your change. It's not so important what you have done, but what you learn from what you have done and how it makes you a better person.

If you're still playing the finger---pointing game, "Oh, why me?" then you are not there yet. Every time you point one finger, three fingers are pointing back at you. Beware that when you do this, you are adding three times the responsibility on yourself to do the right thing.

Now, ask yourself this: *Are you willing to give up bad habits, negative thinking, and negative people? Are you willing to stand up for yourself and fight to the end?*

Remember, God didn't give you the strength to get back on your feet so that you could run back to the same people, places, and things that knocked you down in the first place.

You get out of life what you believe you deserve. What you believe determines what you become.

You have got to stop working so hard at putting your feelings aside, smoothing things over, and ignoring your wants, needs, and desires

I want you to take responsibility for yourself by yourself.
I want you to promise yourself to never, ever, settle for less than
your heart, mind, body, and soul deserves and desires.

One thing I've learned in life is that people are going to talk about you whether you're doing good or bad, right or wrong. If you live your life in fear of disappointing others, you live your life in fear of disappointing you. In the end, you will end of hating yourself, so you must find, create, and learn a new way of thinking before you can master a new way to be.

You've got to get up, look up, and never give up. Don't be afraid to make mistakes. Don't be afraid of rejection. Be afraid when you're not getting up early in the morning to be rejected. Be afraid when you're not putting forth an effort to make something better out of your life. Be afraid when you stop thinking BIG. Be afraid when you start limiting your possibilities. Be afraid when you are not reaching beyond the obvious and not challenging yourself to reach your full potential.

Being rejected is nothing, but to live your life afraid of being rejected, to live your life with no purpose is to die defeated by your own selfish, negative thinking every day.

You need to get up, get out, and get something.
Don't let the days of your life pass by.
You need to get up, get out, and get something.
How will you make it if you never even try?

Outkast

...

Let's take the leaning tower of Pisa in Italy for an example. This tower is one of the most remarkable architectural structures in the world. The building has mystified and amazed people from all over the world. While the tower was designed to be perfectly vertical, during the construction, the tower started to lean due to weak and unstable subsoil.

This is similar to your own life. When you don't have a solid foundation knowing who you are and what you stand for, you begin to lean. You begin to allow your mind to believe all hope is gone. You begin to believe rejection is your reality when rejection should be your motivation to remove those boundaries that you have set up in your mind.

You begin to spend time with negative people and surround yourself in their negativity and idle talk. You convince yourself that you are not capable of achieving your God---given gifts. You find yourself doing nothing but the same things you've already done. Nothing!

In order to get something you've never had, you've got to do something you've never done.

Doing something you have never done requires commitment, a commitment day in and day. I believe it has a lot to do with a person's actions, attitude, and the way they challenge themselves. It is not about the fairness of life, nor the bad decisions and choices you have made. It is about how well you are able to overcome, make a decision to live, and grasp what is before you right now.

In order to get something you've never had, you have to remove anything or anyone that is holding you back from receiving what you want. At times, you will have to make a drastic change, regardless of your circumstances and do whatever it takes to reshape your future. It may mean changing your environment and relocating to another city, maybe even finding a new job or career. Even if it means leaving a relationship or changing a habit, it is your choice to let this thing or person control your outcome.

Think about a time in your life when you had to overcome a crisis. Think about the challenges you faced and the steps you took to overcome that difficulty. As a result of surviving that experience, the next time, instead of giving into negative thinking and blaming problems on external circumstances, you took on the challenge. You took on the opportunity to better yourself and your circumstances. The positive change that took place in your life didn't happen just by chance. It didn't just fall into your lap without commitment. You made a conscious decision to do something you have never done to get something you have never had.

When I think about a time in my life I had to overcome a crisis, I think about the time I was laid off from the very first job I had after 14 years of being released from prison. Being transparent, the very first thing that came to mind was control. When I was a drug dealer, I called the shots. I said how fast, how much and how often, but as fast as that thought popped into my head, the faces of my mother, my children and my future wife appeared.

This was a turning point for me. I had to make a decision to face adversity. It has been said that adversity will either build your character or reveal your character. I'm sure you all can guess I choose to build my character. However, I knew I had to make a drastic decision. I say drastic because after only being home with my family and friends just shy of a year, I relocated two and a half hours away to start a new life with my fiancé in Columbus, Ohio. I needed to make this decision although this was not easy for me. I knew I had to answer to my son and my daughter, but also the one person who stuck by my side those 14 years, my mother.

Staying in the same place was comfortable, but it was also a place full of connections and relationships from my old life. Moving away from that seemingly comfortable place meant a new start, a more stable career, and new relationships. As I mention earlier the process of change involved people, places, and things. While this process for me directly was about places and things, indirectly it affected some of the most important people in my life.

When challenges come your way, it may seem easy for the moment to seek an escape instead of facing your problem. However, when you begin to feed your mind, body, and soul with different stimulants and drugs in order to hide from your problems, they don't just take away from today's problems. Instead, they take away from tomorrow's peace. When you come down off the high, your problems are still right there with you. Some people use food, TV, sex, video games, or gambling to avoid their true reality. We may use these things to hide for a time, but the problem is still there.

Accept yourself as you are now. Start where you are. Accept your flaws and imperfections. Use what you have. Discover your talents. Do what you can. Then, you will begin to see how the world will be amazed and mystified by you, by the changes you have made and will continue to make. Like the Leaning Tower of Pisa, which is imperfect in its perfection, your life will be a monument of wonder because of all that you have overcome. Like the Leaning Tower of Pisa that has defied the odds and the critics, how its strength and beauty has stood the test of time, you also have flaws and imperfections that only serve to make your life more inspiring to the world.

KNOW THY SELF (PERSONAL INVENTORY)

1) *What goals you have put off?*

2) *What are the things you haven't forgive yourself for?*

3) *What are your major goals?*

4) *How do you see yourself?*

Poem: Rise and Fall

By EJ 2013

What goes up must come down.

You can't plant a garden

Unless you plow.

A steady drip of water

Will wear a hole in a rock.

Steadfast in your pursuit of happiness

Will obtain a spot.

BELIEVE in yourself.

RISE

Above the FALL.

One step at a time,

Take your time,

That's all.

"Ball TO YA' FALL" is just a slogan.

Finish what you start.

Never leave nothin' open.

Make the money,

Don't let the money make

You.

Aim before you shoot.

Dreams

Do come true.

It's not about what you possess

But what you can live without.

Success is failure turned inside out.

Whatever you have

Right now

Is the outcome of what you BELIEVE.

The greatest depths

Prepare you to

Achieve.

BELIEVE

Fourteen birthdays, fourteen Christmases, fourteen first days of school, just to name a few of the important moments I missed as my two children grew up without me. However, I never gave up believing that one day I would be there—back in their lives.

Fourteen years later, we are now sharing moments that I always dreamed of sharing together. I was there to see my daughter graduate from high school and enter college at Wayne State University on a track and field scholarship. I was there to see my son, Edward, Jr., turn 21 years old and pursue his dream of becoming a photographer.

The fact that I decided to change and believed it was possible gave me the opportunity to grow and become a productive person.

As I walked toward my freedom at the end of my prison sentence, I knew if I didn't leave my bitterness and hatred behind, I would still be in "prison." I knew that unless I let go of my past, I would end up back in the same place, and I would be again missing out on those moments with my children. It was like taking a leap of faith. It meant I had to learn to trust myself in order to gain true freedom.

BELIEVE IN YOU!

- *Do you feel like you're trapped in a situation with no way out?*
- *Are you willing to get up early, stay up late, and work hard all of the hours in between?*

The first step toward creating a better future, a better you, is to develop the ability to envision it. You've got to visualize yourself going to school. You've got to visualize yourself submitting your resume and getting a good paying job or even the job of your dreams. You need to imagine a career, where you actually enjoy the work instead of a job you're forced to work at because you failed to plan. **People don't plan to fail, they fail to plan.**

You've got to visualize yourself buying a nice car, living in a new house, and buying all the new clothes and shoes you want in life, instead of just window shopping. You've got to visualize yourself, no matter how small the goals or dreams you have, making a conscious effort to obtain it.

When you visualize, you react on your thoughts and what you react on becomes a part of your behavior. If you keep doing it daily with sincere motivation, it becomes a habit, and then it becomes a part of your character.

You may be tempted to debate in order to change another's view, but nothing speaks more powerfully than the things you say and don't do.

After being sentenced to 20 years in federal court, I never once visualized myself doing all of that dead time in prison. I envisioned myself being released from prison before that 20---year sentence was up. Year after year, I acted on that thought by filing appeal after appeal asking for a sentence reduction. Even after I exhausted all of my remedies to file another appeal, it became a habit and a part of my character to keep fighting.

In pursuit of my vision, I wrote the judge a letter asking for a court---appointed lawyer, in spite of the fact that I was told by the courts that I had no legal right to file or ask the judge to rehear my case. Legally, I had a right to have a court---appointed lawyer to represent me in the court of law, but in all actuality, I didn't have grounds to ask for counsel because I had no right to an appeal.

To my surprise and determination, the judge granted my request. My request was granted because of my belief. Belief is a firm conviction of the truth. The truth of the matter was that I was illegally sentenced ten extra years for a felony I had already done time for.

If you don't stand for something, you will fall for anything.

My vision was accomplished by a four---year sentence reduction, and 14 years later I was set free from a 20---year sentence. Ultimately, whatever you have right now in your life, whatever you feel you don't have in your life is the result of what you thought, felt, did, or did not do up until this point. If you want things to be different, you have to speak it into existence. You have to visualize it and believe in the power of your word and your vision.

Believing is being able to visualize the beauty in every situation, even the most dreadful and unpleasant situations. For in every denial in life, there is always a yes waiting if you choose to envision it. If you choose to look at life as too stressful and meaningless to try, you will only see the bad that life has to offer. When you continue to look at the distasteful, nasty, and rotten, the only things you will see in life are the distasteful, nasty, and rotten things that are unpleasant and detrimental to your vision. If you want things to be better, you have to change what you think instead of how you think. You have to change how you feel and envision how you should and want to feel. No one knows your visions, dreams, goals, and aspirations better than you do. Believe in you! Stop working on the approval of others to live out your vision.

Most importantly, you have to change what you do, how you do it, and who you are doing it with. Misery loves company. The company you keep can make or break you. The company of those with limited vision, the company of those with evil intent can and will eventually influence your opinion and actions.

We cannot solve our problems with the same thinking we used when we created them.

That's called insanity. Doing the same things and expecting different results. It's like busting your fist against a stonewall thinking it's going to move.

So, how do you turn a crisis into an opportunity?

You have to believe! You have to find the courage to ask questions and express what you really want. You have to communicate with others as clearly as you can to avoid misunderstanding. You have to avoid idle gossip and negative conversation. You have to change people, places, and things, but more importantly, you have to change your mindset.

You have to get with like---minded people, groups, and organizations. You have to hang around people you know are doing something positive and have positive things to say about life and other people.

Your vision in life is determined greatly by the amount of time you are willing to place in your own thoughts and actions. You have to believe, and I mean truly believe, in your vision. Everything you did in the past has to be redirected to something different, positive, and new. You have to break the cycle of your old ways.

> *To get what you've never had, you have to do something you've never done.*

When you spend two to three hours on social media, you begin to live a fantasy life. When you watch TV (I like to call "Tell lies Visually") all day, every day, you are living out other people's lives, which shapes your perception and productivity.

You have to use your time and energy wisely so that you can equip yourself with the proper tools to overcome any obstacle you may face in life. Productive time management is the key to realizing your vision.

KNOW THY SELF (PERSONAL INVENTORY)

1) *What are the things you wanted to accomplish, but have not?*

2) *What are the projects you have begun, but never completed?*

3) *What things are most important to you?*

4) *What are the ways your thoughts have limited you in achieving your goals?*

BLESSIN' BLOCKIN'

Poem by EJ 2013

When someone do you wrong, they take power over you.

If you never forgive them, then you're BLESSIN' BLOCKIN' too.

Life is too short to carry a broken burden to death.

Forgive them first, then forgive yourself.

Don't live life like you're bulletproof, stuck on pride.

The best kept secret is how you really feel inside.

He who conceals hatred has lying lips,

And whoever spreads slander has a fool's grip.

Ill-gotten treasures are like a gold ring in a pig's snout.

A man shall eat good by the fruits of his mouth.

Given today's hysteria over religion, drugs, and war, Life has no meaning for the under-privileged and poor.

History will continue to repeat itself unless people change.

Judges, politicians, and lawmakers playing the finger-pointing game.

Historically, African-Americans have had to fight for equal opportunity. Don't BLOCK your BLESSIN' with today's possibilities.

Trust me, abundant possibilities will follow you. Life-learned lessons people continue to pursue Like an eagle swooping down on its prey.

You can BLOCK your BLESSIN' if you don't pray.

The fruit of your womb will be BLESSED, The crops of your land won't be a mess.

It's better to give than to receive. It's better to stay than to leave.

You reap what you sow.

Just be better than what you were a week ago.

Experience is the best teacher if you're willing to learn from it.

Finish what you start, don't stop to quit,

BLESSIN' BLOCKIN' your God-given gift.

BECOME

I truly believe that no matter what happens in your life, you can't blame anyone but yourself. Regardless of what happens, only you can allow people, places, and things to control your thoughts, actions, and deeds. I took ownership of my circumstances, changed my behavior, and stopped holding a grudge. I learned that holding a grudge only allowed others to live in my head rent free.

I turned a negative into a positive. I applied myself by traveling the road less traveled and began by believing in myself and putting in the work no matter what it took to become the man I am today instead of the male I was yesterday.

Nothing in life could have prepared me more to become an author and motivational speaker.

...

- *What are you made of?*
- *Do you run and tuck your tail at the first sign of adversity?*
- *Does adversity build your character or reveal your character?*

I'm not going to tell you what to become in life, but I strongly suggest you choose something to become with your life. You will not find what you want to become and what you need to become in life by hanging with the same people, places, and things.

It can be challenging to put distance between the people that are closest and dearest to your heart. It takes effort and commitment to stay away from the places and things that have been familiar to you and the things you have been accustomed to doing day in and day out. However, sometimes doing this will give you a jolt and the motivation you need to be able to truly see what you're made of.

What you're made of consists of more than just your hair, eyes, complexion, height, and size. What you're made of consists of more than the shoes you wear, the clothes you buy, and the jewelry you put on. What you are made of has nothing to do with how many Facebook friends you have. It has nothing to do with you how many people like your picture on Instagram or Twitter.

What have been the things that have been a constant reminder in your life that you can be better?

It should be your values and integrity and the respect you have for yourself and others. The pride and commitment you have when life throws you a curveball should be the rock upon which you stand when you are faced with a tough decision. The rock upon which I stand when I have a tough decision is the gratitude I have for my parents, teachers, and coaches who keep me grounded.

Decision---making is a learned behavior; therefore, you have to accept the responsibility of change as your ticket to your true destiny and purpose in life. You have to do some soul searching and ask yourself what has been your affirmation of your talent and your God---given gifts and abilities. You have to take some time to think on what is your purpose. You have to know your purpose and understand that your purpose is a committed act of effort, patience, and determination.

You have to understand and know that not everyone is with you and for you. In fact, some of the most poisonous people in your life can be the people you trust the most. Until you make the commitment to cut off the people, places, and things that bring you down, life will continue to bring you down as well.

WHAT IS THE OPPOSITE OF SUCCESS?

Falling short of your goals and dreams can be very disappointing, but giving up on your dreams and aspirations in life will destroy your character. You build character by challenging yourself and by never giving up or quitting at the first sign of defeat. Failure is not the opposite of success. Failure is a part of success. Giving up and not trying is the opposite of success.

When I look back at my life, I can't begin to tell you how many times I wanted to give up and just quit. I just didn't have the drive in me after receiving a 20---year sentence in federal court.

The stereotypes that go along with being a drug dealer often led me to believe I couldn't repair my life and rebuild my character. Being a drug dealer has its own set of character traits that I bought into as an inmate for 14 years, yet I held onto a vision of being free even when I had no evidence to support my belief.

` Instead of covering up, tucking my tail with negative self---talk, and giving up on myself because of the stereotypes, I looked at all the beauty still around me, in me, and for me: the beauty of me being healthy mentally, the beauty of me being in good health physically, and the beauty of me having a release date from my incarceration. I took advantage of that beauty to turn a negative into a positive.

I HAD TO DO THE WORK.

During my incarceration I chose to stay up at night while others slept to write six books, over 300 poems, and countless speeches that I now share with other inmates in county jails and correctional institutions. It didn't matter if my fingers would swell and bleed at times. I had a vision and a purpose to overcome the stereotypes I knew I would face once released from prison.

I HAD TO PUT IN THE WORK.

I took parenting classes, computer classes, English and math courses. I read books on productive time management and books on mental toughness. I stayed away from board games, TV, and idle gossip just to stay grounded. **I REINVENTED MYSELF.**

I taught two fitness classes. I organized poetry slams. I educated myself by surrounding myself with like---minded people with similar aspirations. When I was wrong, I didn't make excuses or say things just to get myself out of a jam. I admitted my wrongdoing and apologized for my actions.

It wasn't easy. Change is never easy, yet I did not fear or resist change. I took it on as a challenge to better myself. I embraced it like a newborn baby, innocent and pure. I pursued it with the vigor of a lion chasing after its prey. I kept my head up and spirits high as a coping mechanism to deal with the lonely days and dark nights.

Instead of pointing the finger and playing the blame game, I took advantage of a bad situation and turned it into a positive environment. I took ownership of my bad choices and my bad decisions by acknowledging I was the root of all my problems. I believed that everything happened for a reason. I believed that good things fall apart or things we view as good so that better things can fall together. Things go wrong so that you can appreciate them when they go right. Don't waste your time, thoughts, and energy on people, places, and things that mean you no good. When people do you wrong, they can take power over you. If you never forgive them, then you are blessin blockin, too.

Asking the question, "Why me?" I realized would only keep me in prison long after my release. By focusing on a solution to the problem, I gave myself a chance to turn a crisis into an opportunity.

10% of life is what happens to you.

The other 90% is how you react to it.

The fact is, for 14 years I put in the work while incarcerated. Now as a restored citizen, I gave myself a chance because I made a conscious effort and decision to commit to something other than my past criminal thinking. For example, I got a job and at the same time started volunteering as a mentor at City Readers and at A+ Arts Academy. In addition I was asked to speak to the youth at the Ohio DYS (Department of Youth Services) in Columbus, Ohio and at DYS Cuyahoga Hills.

I made a commitment to stay the course when things got hard and money was low. By making a commitment to change and by putting in the work, I am now a poetic motivational speaker, author, and a facilitator/mentor at MCS---TOUCH (Metropolitan Community Services---Teaching Opportunity Unity by Connecting Hearts) in Columbus, Ohio.

My inner strength combined with believing in myself started me on a journey toward a purpose--filled life of becoming all that I set out to become. Everything I did over the 14 years up until now has prepared me to become the man I am today.

The work, though, is not done. I still have my share of setbacks, hurdles, and obstacles to overcome, but with each challenge I have to anchor myself around like---minded people to help propel me past hardship. Instead of complaining about what I don't have, I thank God for what I do have— life and freedom!

IT COULD BE WORSE.

Once you realize that you are the captain of your life, choices, decisions, and mishaps, you will become and work hard at becoming even more. Now, ask yourself: What do you really want?

KNOW THY SELF (PERSONAL INVENTORY)

1) *What are the things you haven't forgiven yourself for?*

2) *How do others perceive you?*

3) *What does being successful mean to you?*

4) *What are the things you're willing to do to achieve your goal?*

POEM: MY LIFE
Poem by EJ 2014

I took my life, bottled it up, and put it into poetry,

Stitched my past up, rolled it up, and smoked blunts for free.

I am no longer worried about who for me.

Jealousy is misery; suffering ain't for me.

It takes skill to be real, livin' in uncertainty.

Had to learn to hold my own,

Working hard since I was twelve years old.

Pappa never told me the do's and the don'ts.

Not having, I had a greater need to want,

Want what's in those jeans, wanted the money, didn't
want a sister and brother as a crack fiend;
It seems I wanted the American Dream.
The prettiest people do the ugliest things,
Classified as the ugliest of my team.
A college grad, choke my life out for the American
Dream

My life wasn't solid, yet it stood on a solid foundation.
A taste of the streets,
More money, more women, the more I beat my feet.

Gon' 'til November, man, you dudes are clueless.
I never wanted to leave; selling drugs was foolish.

Doing time, I couldn't afford old friends.
All this DAMN stressin', I'm low on dividends.

Even worse, a friend turned me in.

A dose of reality, back to where it all began.

My life is the product of devious grins,

Fake smiles from friends every weekend.

Gone with the money before the week ends.

Winning ain't everything; it's the only thing.

If I ain't winning, I'm losing, chasing a pipe dream.

My life, now put your feet in my Nikes.

A size 12; it's bigger than you like; the price is life.

Thank You

I would like to thank Johnny "Ace" Bryant—as our friendship grew over the years, so did our vision to give back. Thank you for allowing me to give my very first speech with your organization, Higher Learning Education. I want to thank Serena Travis, Les Brown's daughter and my mentor, for giving me a job and helping me with my public speaking. What you gave me and how you coached me has been one of the reasons why I'm able to dig deep and speak from the heart. I want to thank Karyn Alexis for all of your support and introducing me to Tracy Harris. Thanks Tracy Harris for hours of advice on the phone. Whenever I called, you were always there to guide me on what to do to get my book out. Thanks to Brian Woods (MCS–TOUCH) for believing in me and giving me a job to go inside the prisons to speak to the inmates. Thanks to Peggy Watters (MCS--TOUCH) for introducing me to her daughter, Cherie Catron, my editor. Thanks so much, Cherie. Thanks to Matt Moore and the US Probation Department for always calling on me to represent them as one of the most productive restored citizens. I also want to say thanks to my Facebook friends and my YouTube family for all of the feedback on things I needed to be a better speaker and writer. Most of all, thanks to my family, who have been my strongest supporters.

www.ingramcontent.com/pod-product-compliance
Lightning Source LLC
Chambersburg PA
CBHW041306110426
42743CB00037B/10